GET UP AND START A BUSINESS

QUOTES:

"Starting a business is not easy, if it was everyone would do it".

"One year from now you will have wished you started today so get on with it"

"You want your customers to remember you"

"Customer service is key to any successful business"

"Today is the day you start taking life seriously and take your business to the next level"

"Don't fear failure"

"Enjoy watching it come from a small business into an empire"

Get Up and Start A Business

Copyright 2018 by Emma J Biggins

www.emmajbiggins.com

All rights reserved. No part of this publication may be copied, reproduced or distributed in any form including photocopying, recording, electronic or any other mechanic means without prior written permission from the publisher/author. The only form that does not require permission is brief quotes for reviews or other non commercial use.

Contents:

Acknowledgements	6
Intro	8
Chapter 1 – Getting fit	11
Chapter 2 – Figuring Out What You Want To Do	14
Chapter 3 – What Next	20
Chapter 4 – Getting Set Up	24
Chapter 5 – Branding	27
Chapter 6 – Location	42
Chapter 7 – Those First Few Months	45
Chapter 8 – Advertising	49
Chapter 9 – Customer Service	56

Chapter 10 – Appearance	62
Chapter 11 - When You Feel Like Giving Up	66
Checklist	72
Summary	74
Notes and To Do	76
About The Author	103

Acknowledgements:

I would like to thank Max who has helped me to learn so much about business and to push me to be more and do more!!

To all my readers I hope this helps you and inspires you. Thank you!

> CHOSE A JOB
> YOU LOVE
> AND YOU WILL
> NEVER
> WORK A DAY IN
> YOUR LIFE
> Confucius

Intro

This is aimed at people who have not started a business before, they have no idea where to start and could do with a quick guide on what they need to consider. If you have big money then congratulations you can pay people to organise each item mentioned in the chapter´s. If you´re on a budget and need to do more yourself; then be prepared to put in a lot of time and effort to get things moving.

I learned a lot from my partner Max who owns his own business South Spain Properties. I actually helped to rebrand this company. I learned a lot from working on this project. Then I started my own branding company called Business Studio. I noticed that a lot of business books out there are focused at getting rich and making millions. I wanted to write a book that covered the basics, that spoke to the average person wanting to start from scratch. Every idea has to start from somewhere, every business has to start from somewhere. I hope my book will give you the tools and information you need to get out there and create something amazing.

My first book is called Get Up and Start Walking. It helps you to get over negative feelings and reach success. When it comes to starting a business you need to be mentally fit and it will take all of you to get it going. So if you have a lot of doubts or feel like you are not good enough then maybe you need to read that book first.

If you are mentally strong enough to give it all you´ve got and are ready to start on your own business then let´s go.

We are going to go over every aspect. Figuring out what you want to do, how to start off, keeping momentum and what to do when you feel like giving up. It will be like your very own simple to follow guide.

Starting a business is not easy, if it was everyone would do it. It literally does take blood, sweat and tears. You cannot sit back and feel like "well now no one's telling me what to do so I can just enjoy life". It's the exact opposite. When you are trying to get a new business off the ground it takes up more of your time, perhaps you won't even be able to go on holiday for a year or two. It gives you a lot of stress and makes you really learn what hard work really is.

If you haven't been put off yet, congratulations, you need determination and to believe in yourself to win at this game. Anyway let's get to it. Good luck and I wish you all the success in the world.

Chapter 1 – Getting Fit

As I said my previous book took care of preparing you mentally for your dream life. Owning a business requires you to be physically and mentally fit. Why? Because it´s going to take a lot of energy from you. You need your stamina to keep going when others will perhaps have given up already.

When you have ideas running through your mind; it´s easy to just get carried away. One minute leads to an hour, to two, four and before you know it the whole day is gone and you haven´t moved.

Make sure you schedule time aside for working out and meditating or visualising to keep your brain and body in good shape. Be ready to take on any task that may be coming your way.

It is proven that our mental state and physical state is connected and if you go to the doctor with depression they will recommend you getting exercise. Exercise releases endorphins in the brain which triggers a positive energy. This is why exercise is important. Not only will you be physically fit but mentally you will be less stressed and feel more motivated when taking on your day.

Now I know what you may be thinking. You hate exercise. Well I'm not a big fan either but you have to start somewhere. Even if it's just 5 minutes a day, even if it's just a walk to the end of your road and back. Once you start you will feel more energised to do more and it will get easier the more you do it. Be sure to exercise every day for at least 21 days. Why 21 days? Well they say it takes 21 days to create a habit so if you can stick this out for that many days then it should automatically become part of your routine.

Do you have friend that wants to start some form of exercise too? Perhaps you can start together so you can encourage each other.

Busy watching TV every evening? Buy an exercise bike or treadmill and put it in front of the TV so you can do both at the same time.

No excuses exercise is crucial for a successful positive life so start today. You've heard the saying – one year from now you will have wished you started today so get on with it.

Chapter 2 – Figuring Out What You Want To Do

As the saying goes if you enjoy your job you will never work a day in your life.

Perhaps you have decided you want to be self-employed and have your own business, however, you have no idea what you want to do.

The first place to start is to look at your childhood. What did you enjoy, what did you think you´d like to be when you grew up? Are there any clues there? Is there anything you enjoyed that you can bring into your adult life and make money?

For instance to an outside person perhaps it was clear I was a writer but to me I didn´t figure it out until a couple of years ago.

Sometimes we get so caught up in our daily routine and what society expects of us that we lose who we are and what we want to do.

When I was younger I wrote poems. Some were even silly about fireman sam and cartoons I watched.

My mum had an old typewriter and I used to write a lot on there. I would type newspapers with silly news and draw stick people on them (my drawing is not so good). Sometimes I would type utter nonsense that made no sense what so ever.

As well as writing I loved to read, I could lose myself in a book for hours. I also have a good imagination so I thought perhaps I would make a good novel writer so I took a novel writing course. Turned out I wasn't as good at writing novels as I am reading them. I did well in the course but when I sat down and wrote, I couldn't get enough material. Perhaps that's something to try again in the future.

Another thing I really enjoyed as a teenager is reading the agony aunt section in the magazines. For those who may not know what that is, it's the part of a magazine where someone writes in with a problem and then they get advice on what they could do to solve it. I did think I could be an agony aunt as I would come up with good answers and I really wanted to help people.

In the end I ended up working in an office and nothing to do with writing or helping people. A few years back I decided it was time to figure out what I wanted to do. What gave me purpose in life. A book I recommend if you are in the same situation is Finding Your Own North Star by Martha Beck. I read this and it lead me to take part in a beauty pageant. While preparing for this doing charity and doing appearances with my sash I went back to wanting to help people. Social media these days is so full of people posting false photos. They stand a certain way to look thinner or use filters or photoshop. Now I know some people are real and that is really what they look like, but some are just fake and I feel like insecurity and low self-confidence is on the up. So on my journey to the pageant I would only post inspiring photos to my Instagram. If I could help just one person feel better about themselves, then that made my journey worthwhile.

Once I had done my pageant I was back to thinking what now. Anyone who has done a pageant will know that afterwards you kind of come crashing down from the rush. You are feeling a bit down, like it's all over, what am I supposed to do with my time now. I was tempted to just throw myself into another pageant but it just didn't feel like it was the right time. I spend a while trying to just figure out what's next for me. After some soul searching I decided I wanted to help as many people as possible overcome negative emotions and feel good about life and themselves. That is when I started writing my first book Get Up

AndStart Walking. Perhaps you've read it, if so I hope it helped you.

As you can see I went back to my childhood passion for writing, which is why I'm telling you to really think back and remember what you loved to do.

Another option is to think about what you love to do today. What is it that starts a fire inside you and makes you get excited?

Do you have a hobby that you could turn into a business?

The next option to help you is to look at your strengths. What are you really good at? Perhaps it's research, perhaps you are creative, perhaps you are good with organising. Ask people around you, what they think you are good at.

Now put all your information together and see what you have. What jobs can people do with the skills or hobbies you have? Google it if you have to. If you see something that gives an awakening feeling or like you want to learn more then perhaps you found your calling.

Chapter 3 – What Next

So now perhaps you have a clear idea of what business you want to do.

If you don't then don't invest too much time or money in anything, test the water with anything that you found spiked your curiosity from the last chapter. Try out a couple of things on a smaller level and see how much you really like them. Perhaps you decided you might be good at being a nail technician. Before you go ahead and invest go on the internet, research about it more. Perhaps find some friends and paint their nails to see how you like it. If you find you love it, great, if not then move on to the next thing that interests you. Keep doing that until you find what it is you want to do.

When you have found what you like then it's time to do more research. This is where the internet is our friend. Google your chosen topic and find out as much as you can. What do other people in that line of business say? What classes could you take to help you? Do you need qualifications, what investments do you need to make to get started.

Now don´t get disheartened at this point. Perhaps when you see how much work you will need to put in you may start to lose hope. You cannot just say hey presto and then you are living your ideal life with your ideal career. You have to put in the time and effort to learn and raise your knowledge. The more knowledge you have on your chosen subject the more your clients will trust you and feel like you know what you´re talking about.

There may be some bumps in the road and some bends but eventually you will reach the straight and it will get easier. Put in the hard work now to make things easier on yourself in the future.

If you need to take a course then look around to see what fits in better with your current schedule. Perhaps you could do an online course so you can do it at your own pace and in your own time.

Keep searching for YouTube videos and articles on what will help you. Again I'm going to use the nail technician as an example. Look for nail courses in your area. Search on google for tutorials that will help you learn even more. Look at articles from other nail technicians for any tips or advice they can give you. The more information you can collect to help you, the better.

Even when you have got started in business you should never stop learning and researching. You need to keep on top of your game and make sure you are in front of your competitors. The world keep changing and peoples interests keep changing. Things are also constantly improving, so if there is a new technique out there then learn it. Don't just learn it, be the first out there to learn it so you can be ahead of your competitors.

Chapter 4 – Getting Set Up

The first thing you want to do before you start doing anything is check out your competition.

How do they look like they are doing? Are they running successful businesses?Does it look like they are not making money and are in the process of going out of business?

If they are successful, great, that means you have an opportunity to be successful. If they are going out of business you should consider is your idea really worth pursuing. Perhaps there really isn't a market for what you are selling or perhaps other people just don't have your vision or knowledge. This is where you will need to decide is it really worth going forward or should you try another angle. It could be the case that they are going out of business because they are not working hard enough. They don't have good customer service or they are tired and have given up. Don't let their failure put you off if you really have a good vision for your success.

Once you see your competition, learn from them, what is working for them and what could they improve on. What could you offer that they are not so you can gain a good customer base yourself?

Look at their prices, will you offer similar, less to begin with to gain customers or even more because you have a good quality product to sell.

We will talk about how you can ask for more in the chapter all about branding.

Hopefully by now you are getting a good idea of where you are heading. You've checked out the competition and you have an idea of what you are offering. One thing to remember is to keep your product simple. People don't like to be confused. Imagine a restaurant, if they have a menu with many items you start to feel confused and don't know what to order. When they have a select shorter menu, there is usually only one or two that you really could eat and makes your decision much easier.

Be sure to keep writing down your ideas as you go along. Most probably you will go back and forth on a lot of your ideas, it will be a lot to just try and keep in your memory. Be sure to carry a note book around at all times, as you will most likely get ideas popping up at the most unusual times and you don't want to forget them.

Once you have all your ideas together you want to start thinking about a business name, whether you need a website, logos, marketing material, social media and any other ways to launch your new business. I'm going to cover this all in the next chapter called branding as everything you use should be part of "your brand". Everything needs to fit together and let your customers know who you are.

Chapter 5 – Branding

Branding covers a wide range of things so we are going to split them down into sections.

Business Name and Website

First you need to decide if you want a website. These days if people don´t have a website it gives the impression that you are not successful. I would recommend you get one, even if it´s a simple one page website just so people have something to look at. How often when you are searching for a certain product you look them up on websites first. Even if you are planning to start without one until you start making progress, I still recommend buying the domain to make sure you don´t lose the name you want your website to be called. A domain name is simply the name of your website. For example, www.emmajbiggins.com. It is possible you come up with a great name but someone has already bought that domain.

Now again before looking up domains you want to pick your name and alternatives in case that particular domain has already been bought. The best ones of course end in .com as it is much easier for people to remember. However if you are selling a certain product then perhaps an alternative ending is in your favour. For example if you are selling something to do with travelling then your website may stand out with .travel at the end. It also is more likely that the domain will not have been taken yet as like I said .com is the most popular. So think carefully about what your business name is, as people remember your website easier if it is the same as your business.

For example my partner has a business called South Spain Properties and his website is www.southspainproperties.com. Easy to remember for customers and you could also buy other domains to stop anyone having a business with similar name to you. For example if you are selling flowers and your domain is www.flowers.com, perhaps you will also buy www.flowers.co.uk, www.flowers.org, www.flowers.net etc. You will redirect all the others to the .com one. Don´t worry too much about that right now, it´s just an idea and it´s not always necessary. Especially if they are expensive. For the purpose of this book we will stick to just .com.

Now before you start looking at what domain names are available, write down all the possibilities for business names and domains. Call me suspicious but I feel like if you start searching before you are ready to buy, I don´t trust anyone. I am always worried there are people checking what domain names people are searching for. Someone will buy the domain you want in the hopes you will be so desperate for it that you will buy it off them for a higher price. That is why you shouldn´t search for domains until you are ready to buy it as soon as you find the right one.

Once you are set with a list of names and alternatives then you can buy your domain. You don't have to be ready to build a website as long as you have the name, you can leave building the website for as long as you want. A lot of domains if they are not so popular you can buy for as little as $0.99 or $1.99 for 1 or 2 years. You can easily pay for that now then design a website at any point you feel ready.

The website I always use to buy domain names is domain.com but there are plenty out there like godaddy. You can use whichever you want, do a search for buy domain name and pick a site you are comfortable with. All you do is type in the website you want and click search, it will tell you if it is available or not plus a list of alternatives if it is not. Keep going through your list until you are happy with the domain name you have found and follow the instructions to set up an account and buy the name.

Logo and Slogan

Now you have your name and domain set it is time to design a logo and think of a slogan. Think Mcdonalds – I´m Lovin It.

When it comes to business, every little detail needs to tie in together and tell the customer about your business. You want them to remember you and anytime they see your logo or slogan they know who that is. Plus get your brand right and you can charge more for your product. Think Coca Cola vs names that aren´t known. Coca Cola charges more but people are still happy to buy it.

Your logo should tell people what your business is. Again let´s use the example of becoming a nail technician. Your logo is easy, something with nails in it so anyone can see your business is about nails. You wouldn´t put something random in the logo like an elephant (unless maybe the elephant is getting their nails done

:-D). The colours are important too, read the next section about what colours to choose for your business.

Your slogan should say something about your business, make people remember you, make people want to use your service. Think about what you want your customers to know, what can you tell them about your business in a short sentence?

As an example are your products environmentally friendly? This is something you could use in your slogan bringing you more customers who care about the environment. Are you selling food and your product is fresh? Use that in your slogan. Make sure it is factual. If you are saying you're the only company in the area to use farm fresh produce make sure that it is true first. I had a business that took care of branding for people including websites, social media etc. The slogan I used was "bringing your business to life" I wanted to give the impression that I was giving life to a business to make it stand out.

It doesn't have to be anything too fancy. It can be really simple, if you are selling toys perhaps it's as simple as, keeping adults and kids entertained for hours. Whatever it is make sure it tells the customer something about your business. Here are some examples to help you:

Flower shop – Bringing the Bloom to your Home

Nails – A Little Bit of Pampering For Your Hands

Food – Satisfying Stomachs Since ....

Cars – Dreams on Wheels

Fitness – Whipping You Into Shape While Having Fun.

Just be sure to search in Google for your chosen slogan to see if any other company uses it. You don't want to get in trouble for copying.

Colour Scheme

It is so important to pick your colours carefully. Each colour can touch different emotions in people and you don´t want to hurt your business by picking colour that make them stay away from you. Also when you have picked a colour you need to use this throughout your business in future. Your website, logo, marketing, office/shop etc should all incorporate the same colours. This helps the customers identify your brand/business.

Here is a colour guide to help you pick your colours or perhaps make some changes to colours you had already picked.

When using black you don't usually see it used on its own and works well with all colours. Black is associated with power and elegance, think of a businessman in his black suit, you take him seriously and see him as a person high up in his job. You would never use black with cleaning products or food as in chemical products black usually means danger or hazardous and this would put off buyers.

White is associated with Cleanliness and purity. It is used a lot on cleaning products. When talking about safety or hygiene, white is often used, think about doctor's coats.

Red is a very bold colour to use, often associated with love like Valentine's Day but can also be the colour of danger. It also represents energy which is why you often see it on energy drinks. It is used a lot on children's products as this colour triggers the excitement emotion

Blue is associated with trust, loyalty and confidence which is why it is used a lot by banks and finance companies. Also used a lot by companies related to air and sky like airlines; also companies related to the sea and water like cruise ships.

Yellow is a happy joyful colour seen as childish and often used in children's toys. It is also often used in food and sport products. You would never use this to attract a business person, how often have you seen a yellow Mercedes? (A yellow sports car yes as yellow is an attention getter). As yellow is eye catching it can be used to highlight important points of your design.

Green is a very earthy colour so it is used a lot for natural products or environmentally friendly products. You will see it used a lot in farming. Dark green is also a sign of money and is used a lot in banking.

Orange is a bright and cheerful colour associated with sunshine and joy. You would use this colour to draw attention, for example on a call to action button on your website.

Purple is associated with royalty often used in regal clothing. It is also a symbol of wisdom and mystery. You would use this colour if you are selling luxury products.

Pink you see a lot in feminine products like make up or other products aimed at women. It is also like red used as a colour of love. Pink also motivates action and encourages creativity.

Gray is often used as a neutral colour and is seen as calming, Gray is mostly used with another colour.

Brown is another earthy colour and used for organic or agricultural products. Brown is seen as an honest, stable colour.

Gold is a symbol of wealth and success, think gold bullion's. It is seen as valuable and used for expensive items or as a sign of luxury.

I hope this helps you pick what colour scheme you want in your business. Try not to get overwhelmed with all this information. This is just to help guide you.

Business Cards

When designing your business cards, your logo and brand colour scheme should be present.

Now on your business cards, a general rule is you need the name of your business, address, contact number, email and website. If you have other team members then perhaps you will want separate ones, each with your names on, this is entirely up to you. Some like to have their own if they deal with clients individually to give it a personal touch. If you have room you can put your tag line too. However, avoid making it too crowded; people may not bother to read it if there is too much going on. Have a look at business cards you have received in the past or pick some up from any business you go to. Have a look at which catch your eye or which look more professional. Use them as a template for your own. Just be sure to stick to your own brand rather than copying theirs totally.

You can if you like pay someone to design them for you and this will take some stress off you. However, if you want to save money you can easily design them yourself. Vistaprint is one of the more well-known ones. You can search on Google and find which site you can work with best.

Things to remember when designing your business cards are:

1. Is your logo visible?
2. For how many people do you need?
3. Does the place that is printing them require you to send it in a particular file format? (if different printing place from your designer)
4. Make sure all important information is included.

Everything Else

By now you must be clear about your brand so be sure to be consistent with this in everything you do. If you are having flyers made, be sure your logo is present and use the same colours. Everything to do with your business should be easy to identify as yours. Every customer should be able to remember your business. If you have all kinds of different colours, no set logo then they will never remember you. You need a clear consistent brand so that if a customer happens to see your logo while browsing the internet, they will remember you and the experience they had with you.

You want your customers to remember you whenever they see any adverts, social media posts, business cards etc. The way to do that is have your logo and colour scheme on absolutely everything to do with your business. If you have a shop/office, keep the same colour scheme in the decoration and uniforms if possible.

Chapter 6 - Location

Perhaps you will be running your business from home. If you are running it from a commercial building then there are some things to consider. Firstly where is your competition? In the area you are looking at, are there already too many to compete with? Perhaps you will not last long as the competition is too strong. On the other side you should also be careful if there is no competition. There could be a good reason, like this type of business doesn't do well in this area.

Really try to see if there is a gap in the market for what you are offering. Don't be biased because it's your business. Really look into it. Can your product sell, is there a need for it, what sets you apart from everyone else. Do you have a good clear vision for the success of your business? To be honest if you don't see it working out then there is no point even starting. You have to have faith in yourself and your product.

If you are starting at home you have the advantage of no extra costs of renting a building or extra electric bills etc. Perhaps the extra money you save can be put towards advertising and gaining a good client base.

Obviously there are certain business's that cannot be run from home, like a restaurant.

Make sure when choosing a space that you take into account the space you need. You don't want to end up with too big of a space where most of it looks empty. You also don't want a small space that looks too cluttered. Think about all the items you will need. How many tables, storage, do you need a separate kitchen and bathroom area? Get it all down on paper. Even sketch it out. You don't need to be a perfect drawer but getting everything on paper may help you figure out what size space you will need.

Perhaps you know someone with Real Estate experience, or similar that could come with you to look as spaces and help pick one.

Once you have somewhere then you need to buy any equipment needed. What you also need to remember is that although having fancy expensive equipment is impression, you should also stick to a budget and save money where possible.

Chapter 7 – Those First Few Months

So you should be more or less set up now. You have your website and brand set up. You have your location and you are ready to launch.

What the most important thing to remember is; don't wait till everything is 100% perfect to launch. This can be difficult if you are a perfectionist like me. However, if you wait until things are perfect you will never launch!! There will always be an "ooh I could change the style of that" or "Is my business card really professional enough". If you ask any entrepreneur they will agree with me. Do not wait for a perfectly polished end product. Get going and perfect it along the way as you learn more.

The first stages of your business will be like a whirlwind. Say goodbye to deep sleeps and relaxing because you will be awake thinking of ideas. You will also have no free time, if you enjoy having lots of me time then you shouldn't be starting a business. You need to work your ass off to get it to the point where you can let other people run it while you take some time off. Unless of course you're a super millionaire and you can pay people for everything. However, if that is you then I doubt you will need my book. Congratulations to you!!!

You should be promoting your business at every opportunity now. Look for events where you might find people who will be interested in your business. For example, you have a new restaurant and there's an eating competition coming up. Get yourself there, you could find a bunch of potential customers. You have a beauty business, find out about upcoming beauty pageants, wedding fairs or similar.

When you go to any event or network, do not just go to each person, hand out a business card like a flyer and give a sales pitch. People will never remember you, especially if you are not the only one giving them a card that night. People like to hear a story; they like to relate to you. How did you get into this business? What drives you? You want to really connect to people. That way if they need a service that you provide; they will remember you from your conversation and chose you over all the others.

You need to find a common interest with people, make them feel important or interesting. What do you remember about people who try and sell something to you? How can you use this to help your business? This works both positively and negatively. If you remember something you don't like about someone who wants to sell something, think about that when you try to sell to others.

The first few months you may feel out of your depth but don't give up. Keep at it and you will find your feet.

There is no such thing as too much networking. You need to get out to as many places and events as possible. Get the word out that you have arrived and are here to stay. Let them know you and your products are amazing!!!

Chapter 8 – Advertising

The best place to start with advertising is your friends and family. Get them to spread the word for you. Post it on your own social media and also ask them to share it on theirs.

Select some of them that you know will actively talk about your business should the subject come up. Give them some of your cards so they can give them to people when the subject is mentioned. Some people may not bother and throw your cards in the bin, so that is why I am telling you to only use selected friends and family for this one.

Be sure to always take your business cards everywhere with you. You never know when or where you may bump into a potential client, you want to always be prepared.

If you are having separate business accounts on social media, be sure to share on your personal account as well if you have one. Get all (or as many as you can) of your current followers/friends to follow your business accounts too. Be sure to use hashtags in any posts to get more likes/follows. Eg. If you are a restaurant then use #food #restaurant #eatingout and things like that to try and attract more followers. My tip with hashtags is to look at the photo you are posting and basically hashtag everything you can see. With Facebook you don't need to use too many. Instagram you can use up to 30 but with Facebook they say posts get seen more with just a couple of select hashtags.

When posting anything on Social Media you don't want to bombard people with sales posts. Try to stick to the rule of 1 in every 5 posts being sales focused. The rest could be just a nice photo relevant to your business. A quote or anything else that you can think of related to your business. If you have good views from your building then post that. You could always ask customers if they are happy for you to take a photo of them and post that to show you have happy customers. Chances are if they have a social media they will be happy to, especially if you link to their own profile so they can benefit from more follows/likes too.

When it comes to advertising you cannot beat good old face to face. Getting out there and mingling is the best way to find customers. People still prefer a personable face to face conversation. Getting to know who they are buying from and what their story is. People still like to make a connection with the person they are buying from. When talking to people imagine they have a sign over their head saying make me feel important. People will automatically feel a connection with you and want to use your service, if not now, then in the future.

Have a look online or in the paper to see if there are any events coming up in your area where you could benefit from networking there. For example if you are selling clothing then search for any fashion events. If you are selling make up then look for any kind of beauty event, perhaps a pageant. If you have extra time then try any event, even if you don't think it will be fruitful. You never know who you may come across. You can meet clients in the most unusual of places. For example my partner found a client while talking to them in a lift. So don't give up any opportunity for talking to people and casually dropping in what you do for a living.

You could also print out leaflets to give to people or post door to door. Make sure they match your brand and are eye catching. What can you do that will ensure people hold on to your leaflet and not throw it away? Perhaps a discount if they show the leaflet or a free gift if you can afford it.

If you cannot afford any offers then make sure your leaflet really stands out. If you are selling make up then perhaps your leaflet could be in the shape of a lipstick. Or cakes could be in the shape of a cupcake. If you are opening a new gym then print them in the shape of a dumbbell.

Try not to send yourself crazy with all this. It is easy to feel overwhelmed because you want everything to be perfect. When it comes to business you can never wait for a perfect product. As soon as it is good enough then run with it. If you wait until things are perfect it will take too long and you will miss opportunities.

If you have any special events or offers coming up then be sure to spread the word. Via mouth, social media and leaflets if necessary.

When it comes to paid advertising then make sure you think of a budget first. One that you can afford without it affecting your health, stressing you out that you will run out of money.

There are many options on social media now. I recommend starting with a small budget here to see if it works for you and brings actual clients. Make sure you start with small money here so you can play around and try different options of who to target (age group, male/female, etc).

I have heard stories of companies going bankrupt from advertising on social media as they put a high budget on it. This is because you chose a daily limit of how much you want to spend so if you put it too high then you may end up paying more than you want so be very careful here. Perhaps you would benefit from a social media advertising course.

If the thought of tackling advertising on social media scares you then stick to some old fashioned ways for now. Try the local paper or magazines that talk about similar topics to what you are selling. Perhaps there's a local restaurant guide that you can add your own restaurant to.

Try and think of out of the box advertising too. For example if all your competition are advertising a certain way then you do something completely different to stand out. Could you give away a certain product specific to your business with your address etc printed on it? If you sell cars, can you give away some windscreen sun shades with your name on to good clients? If you sell make up can you give away make up bags with your name on to good clients? That way your name gets seen whenever they use your product.

When it comes to advertising, there isn´t really a right or wrong way. Just as long as you're getting your name out there and spreading the word that you exist. Don´t feel like you have to follow everyone else to succeed. Follow your own rules. Who knows you may come up with a brand new way of advertising that is really successful.

Chapter 9 - Customer Service

Customer service is key to any successful business. You need happy customers to not only come back but to tell everyone they know how great you are.

So this is where you need to leave your problems at the door. Your customers do not care if you didn´t get enough sleep, that you just broke up from your partner or that you just crashed your car. Yes life sucks sometimes but as far as your customers are concerned you are happy and helpful.

Always, always greet people with a smile and a positive attitude. Think about experiences you´ve had. If you get treated badly you most likely will never go back nor will you recommend them to anyone else. Even worse you may leave a nasty review online.

Your reputation is everything. Do what you can to keep it a good one. Perhaps your customer is having a bad day and giving you attitude. Tough, suck it up and still smile and be helpful. You never know if they will remember you and bring you more customers in the future.

If they are not satisfied then try and find a solution for them. If you don´t have what they want, is it possible you could source it for them. Have you had a few people asking for the same item that you don´t have, a big sign that you should start selling that item.

Do not take negative comments to heart or personally. Is there anything you could learn from what is being said? Imagine you heard someone saying your chairs look a bit outdated. Before feeling offended and feeling like you are not going to help them one bit. Actually look at the chairs, is there any truth to what they are saying? Could you use some new chairs, do something to update the ones you´ve got? If they are just being awkward and trying to be mean then ignore them. Remember this is business now and you need to stay professional at all times. No matter how difficult it may be.

One thing to consider is your complaints procedure. What is your plan if someone complains? Do you have a complaints book that you can log them? This may be useful as that way you can keep a check on what people complain about so you can take steps on improving. Especially if you have more than one complaint about the same thing.

Do you have an idea of what you might offer someone that complains? Obviously you don't want to lose money on people who like to complain just for the sake of it. However, there may be someone who you feel generally deserves something, like a discount on their next purchase or money off whatever they just bought. Think about how you identify people who have genuine reason to complain to those who complain about anything and everything.

One thing to remember is a lot of people are not looking for freebies; they just want to feel like they are being heard. So let them have a rant if they need to, perhaps once it´s off their chest they will automatically feel better and you won't even have to do or say anything.

Make sure you don´t bad mouth your competition to your customers. If your competition are really not that good, they will work it out for themselves. You bad mouthing them just makes you look unprofessional and/or desperate for them to become your customer.

You also don't want to come across too pushy. No one likes to feel like they are being pressured into buying something. Just be helpful. Give them the information of why they should buy your product. Also try and relate to them. Are they a fan of travelling? Talk about where you last went on holiday to try and build rapport with them.

Also no one can resist a story. What is your story? Share it, use it to connect with people and gain them as a customer. Especially if it is an emotional, moving story. People love things like that. Think about any time you see a story about a cute little animal being rescued. Or someone who tells you a story about overcoming all the odds to be successful. You find it inspiring. You are more likely to buy something off this person who has told you a story, than someone who just shows you a product and hopes you buy it.

Do you have an inspiring story to tell? Have you gone against an important value to chase after your goals? What could you use when connecting with people to help sell your product?

Another thing to remember is if you have staff, to make sure they are trained and that they treat the customers the way you want them to be treated. Perhaps you could even add something to their contract saying if they are caught treating customers poorly that it could lead to termination.

Like I said at the beginning, customer service is key to a successful business.

Chapter 10 - Appearance

Like it or not, appearance is important. You will be surprised at what people noticed and how easily they can be put off.

We still live in an age where we are judged by how we look. People make a decision on whether they like us or not by how we look.

People decided whether they like us or not before we even speak.

Did you know people are attracted to confidence? So the first thing to consider is how you are stood. Be sure to stand tall with your head up and looking confident. If you are slouched in the corner and not making eye contact; customers may feel that you do not know what you are doing and are not confident about what you are selling.

Also the last thing your customers want to see is you hung over from a long night out, looking tired, greasy hair and dirty clothes.

When it comes to business you have to look professional or at least clean. Perhaps you could think about a uniform with your logo on, that way you don't always have to worry about what you are wearing the next day. Make sure it is clean and ironed though.

You would be surprised what people pick up on, especially when it comes to business. When you feel like you did an amazing pitch for your business but they still don't bite. Could it be to do with the fact you got up late and forgot your shower? When it comes to business you can't always use the excuse well they should like me how I am. Sorry but people don't really care, they want to do business with people who are well presented and at least take care of their hygiene. By that I mean you need to do the basics. Get showered, brush your teeth, wear clean ironed clothes and smell good.

If you don't have time in the morning, then get up earlier. Hey remember, if starting a business was easy, everyone would be doing it.

Put yourself in their shoes. Let's imagine you were approached by two different companies but both selling the exact same thing.

The first looked like they didn't have a shower, they had a hole in their jumper and their shoes were covered in mud.

The second looked clean, smart clothes and clean shiny shoes.

It doesn't matter how good the other pitch was you would most likely go for the second one. That is because when people take time to take care of themselves they come across like they take their business seriously. The first person is coming across like they don't really care and are not even bothered if you buy anything.

If you can't even be bothered to take care of yourself why would you be bothered to take care in providing a good quality service.

Remember companies that establish a good service and brand get to charge more. So do you want to be earning little money and get away with looking like a scruff? Or would you prefer to put in the effort to take care of yourself and earn more money?

Today is a brand new day my friend. Today is the day you start taking life seriously and take your business to the next level!!!

Chapter 11 – When You Feel Like Giving Up

Having a business is not easy, especially in the beginning. If it were then everyone would be a successful business person with one or more businesses.

It is hard work and some days you may think why did I bother, I should have stayed working for someone else.

You may be feeling like it's too much, when am I going to see big income, get to go on a holiday or even get some quality me time???

Don't give up just yet; there is a saying that successful people are the ones who keep going when everyone else would have given up.

If you feel like things are getting on top of you then it is important to prioritise tasks and keep a schedule. Keep a calendar and write down everything that you need to do so you don't forget anything important. Also each day make a note of every task that you want to get done. That way you don't have to worry about trying to remember everything you need to get done. You will also feel better as you cross off each task and see how much you are actually getting done.

Make sure you don't try and over work yourself by trying to get too much done in a short time. Set aside a certain amount of time each day for the tasks you want to get done and stick to it. That way you can concentrate on one thing at a time, rather than doing one thing but being distracted by thinking of other things you need to be doing as well.

When you are feeling a bit stressed then just keep yourself focused on the end goal. Remember why you started this and remember what it is you want to achieve.

You can also break down big tasks into smaller ones to make them more manageable and to stop yourself from getting overwhelmed.

Do you know in baseball before the pitcher throws the ball he looks away for a second then throws it. This taking your eye of the ball for a second, refocuses you. Perhaps that's what you need. Take a break and come back to it later. Usually when we are faced with problems the answer comes to us when we stop focusing on it and start doing something else. Ever heard the saying a watched kettle never boils? When you stand looking at the kettle, it feels like it's taking forever to boil. You walk away and it starts boiling. Same with business, take a break and ideas will most likely start flooding back to you.

Any achievement whether it is big or small should be celebrated. When you celebrate your achievements it cheers you on to keep going and achieve more. Plus with all the hard work you are doing, you deserve a treat now and then.

Don't feel bad about taking time out; go back to what I said before about taking your eye of the ball for a bit.

Don't fear failure.

Another really important thing is to not let fear of failure immobilise you.

Firstly there is nothing wrong with failing and you should never look at it as failing. You should see it as a learning experience.

Many successful people have failed before finding what it is that is right for them. So if you do see things going down that road. Do not worry; it's not a bad thing. Perhaps this venture was not right for you; perhaps this was a learning experience to prepare you for something else. Or even perhaps this is the right venture but not the right time, maybe in a few years you will come back to the same project and make it work.

If you are losing too much money or it is seriously affecting your health then maybe it is time to take a step back and re-evaluate what you are doing.

However, do not give up just because it is the easy way out. Do not give up just because you are afraid to fail or even afraid of success.

Push yourself through the difficult times. Success doesn't happen overnight and it happens differently for each person. Perhaps some people will be successful after one year, some five and some maybe more. If you want it hard enough and you put in the work then you will achieve it. Believe in yourself and stay positive. Keep working at it and be sure to enjoy it when it arrives. Some people they work so hard at something for so long that when success comes they carry on working hard and forget to enjoy the moment.

Enjoy the little successes you've had. Enjoy seeing your business grow. Enjoy watching it come from a small business into an empire.

Checklist

To summarise here is a checklist to remind you all the things you need to be considering when starting your business. This is useful if you want to remember certain points without having to go over the whole book again.

1. Get physically and mentally fit.

2. Figure out your passion and explore it, find out more.

3. Check out your competition.

4. Get a good brand. Be sure to use this on anything business related.

5. Select a good location.

6. Don't wait for perfection to launch.

7. Find events to go and network.

8. Advertise everywhere.

9. Customer service is key!!

10. Never stop learning.

11. Take care of your appearance.

12. Don´t be afraid of failure.

13. Remember your achievements.

14. Take you eye of the ball sometimes.

15. Look at the end goal.

16. Enjoy watching your business grow.

Summary.

I hope you liked this book and it gave you a good starting point on getting your business off the ground. As I said in the beginning it is not one of those get rich quick books or how to make a million in your sleep.

It is very basic and straight to the point. It is how to get started and also to help inspire you and point you in the right direction.

I would like to wish you good luck on your venture and hope you have a successful business.

Notes and To Do

I just wanted to add a section where you can make notes.

You can use this for writing down a to do list. Write down points from the book you want to remember.

You could also use it as a space to write down thoughts to help feel better or just try and think of inspiring ideas. Sometimes we can get overwhelmed with thoughts that it makes it easier to just write it down.

Perhaps use the space to writing down your vision for the future or to journal your day to day.

Whatever you use it for I just want to say that writing can really help you get clear on your goals. It can also help get your ideas flowing and get negative feelings out so you can concentrate on making a successful business.

I feel ... Have Achieved... Need ideas ... To Do...

About The Author

Emma was born in Rotherham, South Yorkshire, UK. She moved to Marbella, Spain in March 2011 to be with her soul mate. Here she lives with her dog enjoying walks on the beach. She has studied Business, Novel Writing and Beauty Therapy. In March 2018 she took part in the UK Galaxy Pageant and is in a movie called Hello Au Revoir.Her hopes are to help as many people as possible overcome negative emotions and reach success. To help people live their best life by inspiring and motivating them.

Do you want more for your life but just don't know
where to begin? Feel like time is passing by and your
wasting time watching TV or something else?
Consumed with negative feelings or low self esteem?
Perhaps you would benefit from reading my other
book:

Get Up and Start Walking:

I also have a short poem book that you may be able to relate to or just enjoy:

My Life in Poems:

Find all my books at:
www.amazon.com/author/emmabiggins

Website:
www.emmajbiggins.com

Follow me on social media:

/emmajaynebiggins

@ejbiggins

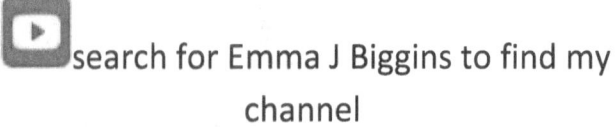search for Emma J Biggins to find my channel